CHOPIN

BARCAROLLE IN F-SHARP MAJOR OPUS 60 FOR THE PIANO

EDITED BY CHARLES TIMBRELL

AN ALFRED MASTERWORK EDITION

Cover art: Venice, from the Porch of Madonna della Salute *(ca. 1835)*
by Joseph Mallord William Turner (1775–1851)
Photo courtesy of Corel Corporation

FRÉDÉRIC CHOPIN
BARCAROLLE IN F-SHARP MAJOR, OP. 60

Edited by Charles Timbrell

Contents

To the memory of the inspiring teachers who taught me
this work—Emil Danenberg (1917–1982), Guido Agosti
(1901–1989), and Gaby Casadesus (1901–1999).

Charles Timbrell

Foreword

Acknowledgements

I wish to thank Ferdinand Gajewski and Christophe Grabowski for helpful information and advice regarding the manuscripts and first editions; Donald Manildi, Curator of the International Piano Archives at the University of Maryland (IPAM), for making available historic recordings and early editions; Jeffrey Chappell, Stewart Gordon, Noël Lee and Brian McManus for valued comments regarding performance problems; the staffs of the Library of Congress, New York Public Library, Howard University Library, the British Library, and the Biblioteka Jagiellonska; and E. L. Lancaster, Vice President / Keyboard Editor-in-Chief of Alfred Publishing, for involving me in the project. Finally, I thank William Kloss for his always patient support and wise advice.

Chopin and the Barcarolle

The *Barcarolle*, Op. 60, is one of the finest works of Frédéric Chopin (1810–1849). Its expressive melodies, rich harmonies and formal perfection have been admired by musicians and writers for many generations. It is sometimes spoken of as his "fifth ballade" or as his greatest nocturne, and indeed it combines aspects of both genres in a unique and memorable way. As Chopin scholar Jim Samson has observed: "It has a mixture of luminosity and strength quite unlike anything else in Chopin's music, but shares with the other very late works a transparency and clarity of expression which points to a plane well beyond technique."[1]

The French word *barcarolle* comes from the Italian *barcarola*, a type of song that the boatmen (*barcaioli*) of Venice improvised as they guided their gondolas and boats (*barche*) through the canals. Johann Wolfgang von Goethe (1749–1832) described them as sounding like a cross between a chorale and a recitative, "the singers changing pitch according to the content of the verse in a kind of declamation."[2] Somewhat later, Franz Liszt (1811–1886) recalled hearing Venetian gondoliers sing the opening lines of Torquato Tasso's *La Gerusalemme liberata* (*Jerusalem Delivered*, 1580) in a plaintive style, giving it "a special character by dragging certain notes, holding back their voices, which, heard from a distance, produced an effect similar to that of rays of light reflected from the waves."[3] Stylizations of such songs—usually in $\frac{6}{8}$ or $\frac{12}{8}$ meter, evoking the movement of a boat on water—were incorporated in numerous 19th-century operas with marine settings, including *Otello* (1816) by Gioachino Rossini (1792–1868), *Oberon* (1826) by Carl Maria von Weber (1786–1826), *Gianni di calais* (1828) and *Marino faliero* (1835) by Gaetano Donizetti (1797–1848), and *La muette de portici* (1828) and *Fra diavolo* (1830) by Daniel-François Auber (1782–1871). In 1828, the popular Parisian composer and pianist Henri Herz (1803–1888) wrote a *Rondo-capriccio sur la barcarolle favorite de la muette de portici*.

Felix Mendelssohn (1809–1847) is credited with composing the first wholly original piano barcarolle during a stay in Venice in 1830. Entitled *Venetianisches gondellied*, it was published as the sixth piece in his *Lieder ohne worte (Songs Without Words)*, Op. 19 (1832).

---

[1] Jim Samson, *Chopin* (New York: Schirmer Books, 1997), 266.
[2] Johann Wolfgang von Goethe, *Letters from Italy*, tr. W. H. Auden and Elizabeth Mayer (London: Penguin, 1995), 43.
[3] Franz Liszt, *Tasso—Lamento e Trionfo* (Symphonic Poem No. 2): *Foreword*, tr. Humphrey Searle (London: Ernst Eulenberg, 1976), v.

In this work, and in two later ones with the same title (Op. 30, No. 6 and Op. 62, No. 5), Mendelssohn melded the characteristics of operatic barcarolles—compound duple meter, a repeating figure in the bass suggesting the lapping of water, melodic writing in thirds and sixths suggesting a love duet, and the use of pedal points—into an idiomatic piano style. Other piano barcarolles followed, including the *Variations quasi fantasia sur une barcarolle napolitaine* (1834) by Charles-Valentin Morhange Alkan (1813–1888) and a transcription of the song *Auf dem wasser zu singen* (*To Be Sung on the Water*) (1837) by Franz Schubert (1797–1828) for piano solo by Liszt. It is significant that the subtitle of the latter work was *Barcarolle* and that its cover featured an engraving of a gondola. Liszt's other early pieces in this style include his transcriptions of the fourth of Rossini's *Soirées musicales*, "La gita in gondola (Barcarola)" (1837), and the barcarolle from Donizetti's *Nuits d'été à pausilippe* (1838). Liszt's rival Sigismund Thalberg (1812–1871) published two transcriptions of barcarolles from Donizetti's operas as well as an original *Barcarolle*, Op. 60 (1839), and Chopin's promising student Carl Filtsch (1830–1845) published a *Barcarolle in G-flat Major*, Op. 3, No. 2 (ca. 1843).

Although Chopin never visited Venice, he was familiar with several of the above-mentioned operas. At his concert in Wroclaw in November of 1830, he improvised on a theme, perhaps the barcarolle, from Auber's *La muette de portici*, and later in the month he attended performances of that opera in Dresden and Vienna. Also during this stay in Vienna, he attended Rossini's *Otello* and Auber's *Fra diavolo*. Unfortunately, it is not known whether he attended a performance of Auber's *La barcarolle, ou l'amour et la musique*, which was premiered at the Opéra-Comique in Paris in April of 1845.

Chopin began composing his *Barcarolle* during the summer of 1845, but it was not a productive period for him and the work remained unfinished in December, when he wrote his family in Warsaw:

> *Now I would like to finish the Cello Sonata, the Barcarolle and something else which I haven't found a title for* [the Polonaise-Fantasy, Op. 61], *but I doubt whether I will have time, for the social rush has begun.*[4]

The *Barcarolle* was finally completed in August of 1846 during the composer's stay at Nohant, a village in central France where he and the French writer George Sand (1804–1876) were spending what proved to be their final summer together at her manor house. Their nine-year relationship had cooled considerably by this time, but they enjoyed pleasant musical evenings with visitors from Paris, including the soprano Pauline Viardot (1821–1910) and the painter Eugène Delacroix (1798–1863). Delacroix wrote to a friend on August 19th that Chopin had marvelously played some Beethoven for him. When it came time for Delacroix to return to Paris at the end of the month, Chopin entrusted him with a valuable package: the manuscripts of the *Barcarolle*, Op. 60, the *Polonaise-Fantasy*, Op. 61, and the *Two Nocturnes*, Op. 62. Delacroix was asked to deliver them to Auguste Franchomme (1808–1884), Chopin's cellist-friend in Paris, who would disperse them to publishers.

In his cover letter to Franchomme, dated August 30, Chopin wrote:

> *My very dear friend,*
>
> *Here are 3 manuscripts for Brandus, 2 and 3 for Maho* [the Paris representative for publisher Breitkopf & Härtel], *who will pay you the money from Härtel (1,500 fr.). Don't give up the manuscripts until the moment of payment. Send me a note for 500 francs in your next letter, and keep the rest for me. I am giving you a lot of trouble; I wanted to avoid it by going to Paris myself this month but—but—but—. Ask Maho not to change the manuscripts intended for Härtel, because, as I will not be correcting the Leipzig proofs, it is important that my manuscript should be clear. Also, tell Brandus to send me two proofs, so that I will be able to keep one.… I will never finish* [writing this letter] *if I start gossiping with you… Eugène Delacroix, who kindly offers to take charge of my message to you, is about to leave…*[5]

On the same date, Chopin addressed a package to another friend, the Paris banker Auguste Léo, who often acted as his intermediary with the London publisher Wessel. The cover letter to Léo reads:

> *…I thought of bringing my manuscripts to Paris, but the beautiful season makes me stay, and I'm going to bother you*

[4] *Correspondance de Frédéric Chopin*, ed. and tr. Bronislas E. Sydow, Suzanne Chainaye, and Denise Chainaye (Paris: Richard-Masse,

1959), III: 225 (letter of 12-26 December 1845).
[5] Ibid., 238-39 (letter of 30 August 1846).

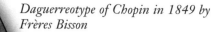

Daguerreotype of Chopin in 1849 by Frères Bisson

with my parcel for London. As you are usually kind enough to send at the same time a bill to be paid two months later, please send it to me to sign if it's absolutely necessary. The price will go up this time to 30 pounds.[6]

Given the date of this package, its contents and its Paris destination, it seems likely that Delacroix conveyed it along with the package for Franchomme.

On September 9, Chopin wrote Léo that he was "eager to return Wessel's contract"[7] and on the 13th he wrote Franchomme:

I am very angry that Brandus is away and that Maho is not yet able to receive the manuscripts that he often asked me for this winter. One must wait, therefore, but I beg you to kindly return there as often as seems possible, because I would not like this affair to drag on, having sent my copy to London at the same time as to you.[8]

On September 22, Chopin again wrote Franchomme, this time thanking him for meeting Maho and for sending him the money from Brandus. He added that "the date chosen for publication seems excellent, and I only have to ask you to watch that Brandus doesn't fall asleep on my account."[9]

Thus, we know that by August 30, Chopin had prepared a total of nine manuscripts, three copies each of Opp. 60, 61, and 62. The reason for this was his wish to achieve simultaneous publication in different countries, the publishers for these works being Brandus et Cie. in Paris, Breitkopf & Härtel in Leipzig, and Wessel and Co. in London. This practice, which was common at the time, allowed composers to prevent their works from being pirated by unscrupulous publishers.

The first edition of the *Barcarolle* was Wessel's, which was registered at Stationer's Hall on October 7 and deposited at the British Museum on October 13.[10] Chopin had neither requested nor received proof copies from Wessel. Brandus sent Chopin proofs of their edition by October, and they announced its publication in the Paris press on November 8 and registered it at the Bibliothèque Nationale (*Dépôt légal*) on November 13.[11] On November 11, Chopin returned to Paris from his five-month stay at Nohant, and a few days later he wrote Breitkopf & Härtel to acknowledge receipt of their payment for Opp. 60, 61, and 62.[12] Their edition of the *Barcarolle*, of which Chopin did not request or receive proofs, appeared before the end of the year, probably in November. All three editions are dedicated to Chopin's friend Madame la Baronne de Stockhausen. Her husband, the Hanoverian ambassador in Paris, had been the dedicatee of Chopin's *Ballade in G Minor*, Op. 23. (See "About This Edition" for further discussion of the manuscripts and first editions.)

Chopin performed the *Barcarolle* at his final concert, at the Salle Pleyel on February 16, 1848. Although quite ill, he was said to have played beautifully. The program also included some of his preludes and mazurkas, a waltz, a nocturne, an étude, the *Berceuse*, Op. 57, the last three movements of his Cello Sonata, Op. 65 (with Franchomme) and a Mozart piano trio. The pianist Charles Hallé (1819–1895), who attended this concert, remembered some years later that:

Chopin played the latter part of his Barcarolle, *from the point where it demands the utmost energy* [measures 84 ff.], *in the most opposite style,* pianissimo, *but with such wonderful nuances, that one remained in doubt if this new reading were not preferable to the accustomed one. Nobody but Chopin could have accomplished such a feat.*[13]

---

[6] Ibid., 239 (letter of 30 August 1846).

[7] Ibid., 241 (letter of 9 September 1846).

[8] Ibid., 241 (letter of 13 September 1846).

[9] Ibid., 243 (letter of 22 September 1846).

[10] Information kindly supplied in a communication from Dr. Christophe Grabowski, dated 11 January 2005.

[11] Christophe Grabowski, "Les éditions originales de Frédéric Chopin," *Revue de musicologie* 82, no. 2 (1966), 225.

[12] *Correspondance*, III: 254 (letter of 19 November 1846).

[13] C. E. and Marie Hallé, *Life and Letters of Sir Charles Hallé, Being an Autobiography (1819-1860) with Correspondence and Diaries* (London: Smith & Elder, 1896), 36.

Form, Interpretation, and Style

The tightly-knit structure of the *Barcarolle* has several elements in common with sonata-allegro form. As the following diagram demonstrates, the sequence of keys moves from the tonic to the lowered mediant (major), then to the dominant, and finally back to the tonic. The return to the tonic coincides with the recapitulation of the three main themes.

Measure	Material	Key	Tempo
1–3	Introduction	F-sharp	Allegretto
4–34	Theme A	F-sharp	
35–38	Transition		Poco più mosso
39–61	Theme B	A	
62–71	Theme C	A	Poco più mosso
72–77	Transition		Meno mosso
78–83	Theme D	C-sharp	
84–92	Theme A	F-sharp	Tempo primo
93–102	Theme C	F-sharp	Più mosso
103–110	Coda (Theme B)	F-sharp	Tempo primo
111–116	Codetta	F-sharp	

This is not to suggest that the work is in sonata, sonatina or rondo form. The unique, organic nature of the form is intimately tied to the music's strong narrative quality. The opening measures gain the listener's attention by a bold change of register and an unre-solved dominant-ninth harmony followed by a half measure of silence. Then, the barcarolle rhythm is stated simply and in the same "once-upon-a-time" mood as at the start of each of the four ballades. As with the ballades, we do not know what the program or "story" might have been, if indeed there was any.

Jim Samson has rightly observed that variation is "the life blood of [the *Barcarolle*], as of many of the late pieces, and it ranges from the ornamental elaboration of minor details to the transformation and 'enlargement' of extended paragraphs."[14] Each theme is first stated quietly and then elaborated upon. Time seems suspended during measures 72–77, a transition that ushers in the brief but beautiful D theme. This nocturne-like passage provides a change of key and texture as well as some relief from the insistent barcarolle rhythm. Then, each theme is strongly restated and supported by increasingly rich harmony, with a fragment of the B theme treated sequentially in the ecstatic coda.

---

[14] Samson, 266.

The association of barcarolles with romance was so well established in operas that it is not surprising to learn that the pianist Carl Tausig (1841–1871), one of Liszt's favorite students, had a fanciful romantic program for the *Barcarolle*. When he played the work for Wilhelm von Lenz (1809–1883), Tausig observed:

It tells of two persons; of a love scene in a secret gondola—we might even call it symbolic of lovers' meetings in general. That is expressed in the thirds and sixths. The dual character of two notes—or two persons—runs through the whole; it is all two-voiced, or two-souled. In the modulation into C-sharp Major (marked dolce sfogato)*, you can recognize a kiss and an embrace—that is plain enough.*[15]

Von Lenz, a cultured amateur musician who had studied with Chopin, was completely won over by Tausig's performance of the work:

How difficult, how impossible, except to subjective interpretation, it is to carry through nine pages of enervating music, in the same long-breathed rhythm…so much interest, so much emotion, so much drama, and so much action, that I regretted only that the long piece was not longer.[16]

Later in the century, the *Barcarolle* was performed by many leading pianists, including Clara Schumann (1819–1896), Anton Rubinstein (1829–1894), Hans von Bülow (1830–1894), Karl Klindworth (1830–1916), Camille Saint-Saëns (1835–1921), Sophie Menter (1848–1918), Vladimir de Pachmann (1848–1933), Annette Essipova (1850–1914), Teresa Carreño (1853–1917), Ignacy Jan Paderewski (1860–1941), Moritz Rosenthal (1862–1946), Ferruccio Busoni (1866–1924) and Leopold Godowsky (1870–1938). According to James Huneker (1860–1921), Rubinstein "did all sorts of wonderful things with the coda of the *Barcarolle*" and played the *forte* passages *pianissimo*, just as Chopin had done on his last recital.[17]

The *Barcarolle* was also one of the favorite works of the philosopher Friedrich Nietzsche (1844–1900), who first heard it performed in Basel by Hans von Bülow. Thereafter, he often asked his friend Peter Gast to play it for him during their meetings. In March of 1880, Gast wrote in his memoires:

Nietzsche came to see me Tuesday and I played Chopin's Barcarolle *for him, in my best manner, several times over. We cannot get enough of these charming sounds, of the fantastic richness of all that is implied in them, of its perfection of form.*[18]

In the same year, Nietzsche wrote:

Almost all conditions and ways of life have a blissful *moment, and good artists know how to fish it out….This blissful moment Chopin has, in his* Barcarolle, *expressed in sound in such a way that the gods themselves could on hearing it desire to spend long summer evenings lying in a boat.*[19]

The writer André Gide (1869–1951) was a good amateur pianist who was almost obsessed with the *Barcarolle*. His book *Notes sur Chopin* contains three memorable passages about the work:

Before Debussy and certain Russians, I do not think that music was ever so shot through with the play of light, with the murmur of water, with wind and foliage. Sfogato, he wrote. Has any other musician ever used this word, would he have ever had the desire, the need, to indicate the airing, the breath of breeze that, interrupting the rhythm, comes unexpectedly to freshen and perfume the middle of his Barcarolle?…

Returned to Chopin's Barcarolle, *which is not as difficult to play more quickly as I had thought… But in this way it loses all character, all emotion, all* languor; *and it's that above all that this admirable work expresses: languor in excessive joy. It seems that there is too much sound, too many notes once one no longer understands the perfect significance of each one of them.*

[15] Wilhelm von Lenz, *The Great Piano Virtuosos Of Our Time*, ed. Philip Reder (revised translation of *Die Grossen Pianoforte-Virtuosen unserer Zeit as persönlicher Bekanntschaft*) (London: Kahn & Averill, 1983), 71.
[16] Ibid.
[17] James Huneker, *Chopin: The Man and His Music* (New York: Dover Publications, 1966), 54.

[18] Georges Liébert, *Nietzsche and Music*, tr. David Pellauer and Graham Parkes (Chicago: University of Chicago Press, 2004), 184.
[19] Friedrich Nietzsche, *The Wanderer and His Shadow* [second supplement to *Human, All Too Human*], tr. R. J. Hollingdale (Cambridge: Cambridge University Press, 1996), 347.

The Barcarolle *and the* Berceuse…*are two of my favorite Chopin pieces and I am inclined to put the* Barcarolle, *as Nietzsche did, at the pinnacle of his* oeuvre…*These two works are steeped in an extraordinary joy: the* Berceuse *in a tender and quite feminine joy; the* Barcarolle *in a kind of radiant, graceful and robust lyricism that explains Nietzsche's predilection…and mine.*[20]

Nearly 100 barcarolles for the piano were published between 1850 and 1900, including five by Chopin's friend and neighbor Alkan, six by Anton Rubinstein, one by Peter Tchaikovsky (1840–1893), one by Josef Hofmann (1876–1957), and two by Sergei Rachmaninoff (1874–1943). Among 20th-century barcarolles, mention should made of those by R. Nathaniel Dett (1882–1943), Béla Bartók (1881–1945), Alfredo Casella (1883–1947), Charles Griffes (1884–1920) and Ned Rorem (born 1923).

It was in France at the turn of the century that Chopin's *Barcarolle* had its strongest influence, most notably in the 13 barcarolles by Gabriel Fauré (1845–1924), a series that spans his entire career. The large-scale *Barcarolle No. 5 in F-sharp Minor*, Op. 66, is perhaps the closest in spirit and technique to Chopin's, including its key (the parallel minor of Chopin's), long phrase lengths, strong chordal climaxes, scale passages, tonal centers related by thirds, sequences, powerful coda, and peaceful codetta.

Claude Debussy (1862–1918) studied piano as a child with a Mme. Mauté de Fleurville, who claimed to have studied with Chopin, and his later teacher at the Paris Conservatoire was Antoine Marmontel (1816–1898), who had often heard Chopin play. Debussy studied many of Chopin's works and eventually edited all of them for Durand (published in 1916). One of Debussy's early piano students was Mme. Gérard de Romilly, who left an amusing account of her lessons:

Chopin's Barcarolle *was one of his favorite pieces, and it was the cause of violent scenes between us! I played Chopin very badly, and particularly the* Barcarolle, *which I had taken a dislike to ever since Debussy insisted on my repeating it a considerable number of times: "You will work at it until you can play it well," he said, "for years if necessary." The way he explained and analyzed*

the piece was admirable, not bothering about details, only about the overall performance. When we got to the passage where the tune is heard in force, accompanied by ever more powerful octaves in the left hand, Debussy would sing and puff; you'd think he was pushing the gondola himself, and this energetic interpretation would end, thanks to my clumsiness, in general despair.[21]

Debussy did not write barcarolles by name, but almost all of his water-pieces—above all, *L'isle joyeuse*—owe a debt to Chopin's work.[22]

Maurice Ravel (1875–1937), who throughout his life was greatly influenced by the piano writing of Liszt, nonetheless had a keen appreciation of the special qualities of the *Barcarolle*:

(Chopin's) inspired passage work may be observed amidst brilliant, exquisite, and profound harmonic progressions… In the Barcarolle, *the theme in thirds, supple and delicate, is continually arrayed in dazzling harmonies. The melodic line is continuous. At one point a gentle melody appears, remains suspended, and subsides softly, underpinned by magical chords.*[23]

A clear lineage runs from Mendelssohn's three pieces entitled *Venetianisches gondelleid* through Chopin to Fauré and up to the recent *Two Barcarolles* (1993) by the American composer David Diamond (1915–2005). Along the way, Johannes Brahms (1833–1897) demonstrated his admiration for Chopin's *Barcarolle* on the final page of his *Sonata in F-sharp Minor*, Op. 2 (composed in 1852), where the key, tempo, dynamics, filigree, and final descending scale ending with dominant-to-tonic chords are too similar to be coincidental. Many years later, Brahms edited the *Barcarolle* for Breitkopf & Härtel.

[20] André Gide, *Notes sur Chopin* (Paris: L'Arche, 1949), 12-13; 52; 103-104.

[21] *Debussy Remembered*, ed. Roger Nichols (Portland, Oregon: Amadeus Press, 1992), 55.

[22] For a penetrating discussion of Chopin's music in relation to that of Fauré and Debussy, see Roy Howat, "Chopin's influence on the *fin de siècle* and beyond" in *The Cambridge Companion to Chopin*, ed. Jim Samson (Cambridge: Cambridge University Press, 1992), 246-283.

[23] Maurice Ravel, "Les Polonaises, les nocturnes, les impromptus, la Barcarolle—Impressions," *Le Courrier musical*, 1 January 1910, 31-32, as translated in *A Ravel Reader*, ed. Arbie Orenstein (New York: Columbia University Press, 1990), 336.

About This Edition

Primary and Secondary Sources

In this edition, all parenthetical material is editorial. The five extant primary sources used in the preparation of this edition are:

• first autograph, or composing score, located in the Biblioteka Jagiellonska in Kraków, Poland (without catalogue number). It served as the engraver's copy for the first French edition. It was owned successively by Chopin's Scottish pupil Jane Stirling, his Norwegian pupil Thomas Tellefsen, and the French Chopin scholar Edouard Ganche before it was acquired by Polish collectors around 1943.[24]

• later autograph, or fair copy, located in the British Library, London (Zweig MS. 27). It served as the engraver's copy for the first German edition. In 1877 it was lent by Breitkopf to Brahms, who was editing the work as part of Breitkopf & Härtel's Chopin *Gesammtausgabe*. It was then acquired by Clara Schumann and inherited by her grandson, Robert Sommerhoff, who sold it in 1932 to the writer Stefan Zweig, whose collection was acquired by the British Library in 1986.[25]

• first English edition, published in London by Wessel & Co. (pl. no. 6317)

• first French edition, published in Paris by Brandus et Cie. (pl. no. 4609)

• first German edition, published in Leipzig by Breitkopf & Härtel (pl. no. 7545)

Two secondary sources were also used:

• copy of the first French edition with Chopin's annotations, from the collection of his student Camille Dubois (*née* O'Meara), located in the Bibliothèque Nationale, Département de la Musique, Paris (Rés. F. 980, vol. 3)

• copy of the first French edition with Chopin's annotations, from the collection of his student Jane Stirling, located in the Bibliothèque Nationale, Département de la Musique, Paris (Rés. Vma 241, vol. 6)[26]

The first autograph consists of eight leaves (seven written sides) and includes many crossings-out and corrections. A somewhat later autograph, now lost (the one Chopin sent via Auguste Léo to the English publisher Wessel), was based on the first one but, to judge from the Wessel edition, included quite a few changes. The later extant autograph, consisting of eight leaves (seven written sides), was based on the lost autograph and is an extremely neat manuscript with few corrections but some oversights.

On the whole, the first editions are reasonably accurate reflections of the autographs on which they were based (some deductions are necessary in the case of the Wessel edition). The Brandus edition was the only one to benefit from Chopin's corrections prior to publication, but since his autographs were no longer available to him, he must have done the proofing against his sketches or from memory. In any case, his corrections were few (see "Critical Commentary" for measures 6, 32, 40, 50, 76, 78, 83, 89, and 100).

Of the secondary sources, the Dubois copy is of interest particularly because of Chopin's indications for performing grace notes on the beat in measures 34 and 51 and for the changed slurring in measures 102–103. The Stirling copy contains added slurring or note corrections in measures 31, 47–48, 59–60, 92, 96, and 114.

---

[24] Krystyna Kobylanska, *Frédéric Chopin: Thematisch-Bibliographisches Wekverzeichnis* (Munich: G. Henle, 1979), 130. This autograph has been published in a facsimile edition as *Fryderyk Chopin: Barkarola*, preface by Wladyslaw Hordynski (Kraków: Polskie Wydawnictwo Muzyczne, 1953).

[25] Arthur Searle, *The British Library Stefan Zweig Collection: Catalogue of the Music Manuscripts* (London: British Library, 1999), 31-32. Kobylanska (above, 131) lists as lost an autograph that once belonged to the dedicatee of the *Barcarolle*, whose daughter Elizabet von Herzogenberg wrote Brahms in 1877 that her brother would like to give it to him. It seems unlikely that Chopin would have produced four autographs of this work and more likely that it has somehow been confused with the one now in the British Library.

[26] This source has been published as part of *Frédéric Chopin: Oeuvres pour piano: Fac-similé de l'exemplaire de Jane Stirling avec annotations et corrections de l'auteur*, introduction by Jean-Jacques Eigeldinger, preface by Jean-Michel Nectoux (Paris: Bibliothèque Nationale, 1982).

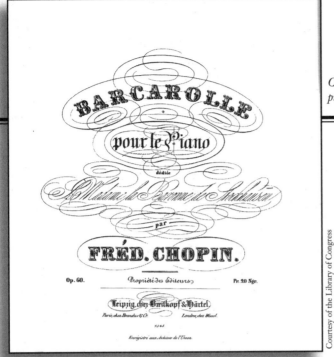

Cover of the first German edition by Breitkopf & Härtel, published in late 1846

The main editorial problems arise from the fact that Chopin knowingly sent out three autographs that differed in many details, apparently seeing no need to bring them into agreement. Chopin scholar Jeffrey Kallberg has summarized the situation as it applies to a short passage in the *Nocturne in B Major*, Op. 62, No. 1, but it applies equally to problems encountered in the *Barcarolle*:

> *The Brandus edition clearly represents the chronological "final" version [because it was proofread by Chopin], which might suggest that it should serve as the basis for a modern edition. But it does not quite agree with the German or English editions; Chopin's memory while making the changes in the French proofs may have been faulty. That is, when Chopin shipped off the German and English autographs, he presumably also thought of these as "final" versions. So we are left with at least two "final" versions of this passage, one represented by the German and English sources, and one by the French edition. Even if we depend solely on the concept of "composer's intentions" to solve editorial problems, we would still be confounded in this instance. Where do we locate Chopin's "final" intentions?*[27]

Kallberg's conclusion is that in certain cases there can be equally authoritative versions for a Chopin work and that for a modern editor to publish only one of them "would be to deny the validity of the arrangements [between composer and publisher] that yielded the other."[28]

The present edition is based primarily on the later autograph, because of its neatness and its generally more refined readings. This source, however, is not free of errors and oversights (as early as measure 1) and for this reason certain authoritative readings have been included from the first autograph, the proofread Brandus edition, and the Wessel edition (based on the lost second autograph).

Later Editions

The following editions were also consulted (listed chronologically): Karl Klindworth (Moscow: Jurgenson, 1873–76); Chopin *Gesammtausgabe*, Vol. 10 (Leipzig: Breitkopf & Härtel, 1879); Carl Mikuli (Leipzig: Kistner, 1879–80); Hermann Scholtz (Leipzig: Peters, 1879); Eduard Mertke (Leipzig: Steingräber, 1880); Theodore Kullak (New York: G. Schirmer, 1882); Ignaz Friedman (Leipzig: Breitkopf & Härtel, 1913); Claude Debussy (Paris: Durand, 1915); Louis Diémer (Paris: Lemoine, 1916); Rafael Joseffy (New York: G. Schirmer, 1916); Emil von Sauer (Mainz: Schott, 1918); Edouard Ganche (Oxford: Oxford University Press, 1932); Alfred Cortot (Paris: Sénart-Salabert, 1936); Ignacy Jan Paderewski, Ludwik Bronarski, and Józef Turczynski (Kraków: Polish Music Publications, 1962); Maria Gambaryan (Moscow: Musica, 1974); Ernst Herttrich (Munich: G. Henle, 1978); and Jan Ekier and Pawel Kaminski (Warsaw: National Edition of the Works of Frédéric Chopin, 1992 and 2002).

Brahms's edition for the Chopin *Gesammtausgabe* is based on the first German edition but incorporates some readings from the first French edition. Mikuli, a former student of Chopin's, based his edition on the first French one. Of the editions by Liszt's students (Klindworth, Kullak, Joseffy, and Sauer), Kullak's may be the best, containing the fewest editorial interpolations. The Ganche edition relies exclusively on the first French edition and Jane Stirling's annotated copy of it. Cortot's edition is of interest for its pedagogical and interpretive advice. The so-called "Paderewski edition," edited primarily by Bronarski, mixes the primary sources freely and cites only the first of the two autographs. The editions by Herttrich and the second edition by Ekier and Kaminski are more scholarly, although their critical commentaries are somewhat abbreviated.

---

[27] Jeffrey Kallberg, *Chopin at the Boundaries: Sex, History, and Musical Genre* (Cambridge: Harvard University Press, 1996), 220.
[28] Ibid.

Performance Issues

Ornamentation

Regarding trills, Mikuli observed that Chopin "mostly began them with the [upper] auxiliary note."[29] In his edition of Chopin's complete piano works, however, Mikuli's trill fingerings often begin on the principal note. In the absence of first-hand information from Chopin's other students, this editor usually favors beginning the trills in the *Barcarolle* on the principal note. The reasons for this are evident from the musical contexts, where a smooth elision with the preceding melodic note is desirable. Also, it should be observed that Chopin's rare fingerings for trills in the autographs of the *Barcarolle* suggest that beginning them on the auxiliary is the exception rather than the rule.

Grace notes should generally be played before the beat, so that they contribute to the flowing character of the melody. This practice is followed on recordings of this work by such noted Chopin players as Vladimir de Pachmann (1848–1933), Alfred Cortot (1877–1962), Arthur Rubinstein (1887–1982), Benno Moiseiwitsch (1890–1963), Vladimir Horowitz (1903–1989), Shura Cherkassky (1909–1995), and Jan Ekier (born 1913), among others. Chopin's pedaling in measure 111 also confirms this practice. Grace notes played on the beat would often interfere with the rhythms in the left-hand part, and in measure 86 such an execution would be physically impossible for many pianists.

On the other hand, arpeggiated chords (as in measure 8) and grace notes written before strong beats (as in measure 10) should be played on the beat, so that the harmony they provide is caught by the pedal. In measures 34 and 51 in the Dubois copy referred to above, Chopin drew lines to connect right-hand grace notes with the corresponding left-hand strong beats. In the present edition, these two instances are indicated by solid lines. Related instances are indicated by editorial dashed lines, as are the lines from arpeggiated chords.

Pedaling

This editor has performed the *Barcarolle* several times on a restored Pleyel grand piano of 1844 and can verify that Chopin's indications for the damper pedal are well suited to that instrument. Modern pianists should bear in mind that printing conventions during Chopin's time prevented the indication of syncopated pedaling, for the sign used to indicate the raising of the pedal (*) always had to be printed a certain distance before the next pedal ("Ped.") sign. Also, it should be noted that the absence of pedaling in the autographs does not necessarily mean that Chopin wanted none to be used. (The first such places are at the end of measure 1 and the beginning of measure 2).

In general, Chopin's pedal indications in the British Library autograph are more precise and refined than those in the earlier Kraków autograph. For example, in measures 16 and 17 in the earlier autograph, his pedal changes occur on the strong beats, but in the later autograph they occur on weak beats in order to assure that the appoggiaturas (non-harmonic tones on strong beats) are not caught by the pedal. However, even the later autograph contains lapses and ambiguities.

For these reasons, two sets of pedaling are given in this edition: the upper one being Chopin's as it appears in the British Library autograph, and the lower one being this editor's. (Neither set includes indications for the use of the *una corda* pedal, which Chopin is known to have used quite often, even though he never indicated it in any of his autographs.) Ultimately, the performer must use the damper pedal according to what the ear, the instrument, and the acoustics dictate. On large instruments, shallow pedaling should be considered for the climactic passages.

---

[29] Jean-Jacques Eigeldinger, *Chopin: Pianist and Teacher As Seen by His Pupils*, tr Naomi Shohet, Krysia Osostowicz, and Roy Howat, ed. Roy Howat (Cambridge: Cambridge University Press, 1986), 58-59 and 131-134. See also Mikuli's preface to his edition of Chopin's complete piano works (Leipzig: Kistner, 1879, reprinted New York: G. Schirmer, 1916).

Dynamics

In many Chopin autographs there are instances of what appear to be redundant dynamic markings—that is, *dim.* or *cresc.* appearing next to or within a diminuendo sign or a crescendo sign (hairpin). The implications of these seeming redundancies have been explored in recent publications by Eric Heidsieck and Seymour Bernstein, who conclude that Chopin often seems to have used the signs to signify brief changes of motion (*accelerando* or *rallentando*) while the simultaneous abbreviations *dim.* or *cresc.* were used unambiguously to indicated dynamics.[30] In the interest of clarity, this edition does not reproduce such double indications. Instead, they are mentioned in the "Critical Commentary" for measures 24, 32, 50, 54, 58, and 61.

Accents

Related to the above consideration about dynamics is the matter of Chopin's use of accent signs of varying lengths in his autographs. The Chopin scholar Jean-Jacques Eigeldinger has suggested that "short accents" were used to indicate conventional accents, whereas "long accents" (which resemble diminuendo signs or hairpins) may have served various functions:

> ...to indicate dynamic reinforcement, expressive stress and proportional prolongation for notes of long rhythmic value; to convey a sense of "leaning" to appoggiaturas, suspensions and syncopations; to emphasize groups of two, three or four notes, as well as chords; and to prolong a stress over tied notes.[31]

Because this area of research is a relatively new one, and because the lengths of accents vary between the two autographs of the *Barcarolle*, no attempt has been made to differentiate them in the present edition. Instead, all accents except those in measures 21 and 31 are printed as short ones, and the differences are mentioned in the "Critical Commentary."

Fingering

The fingering is the editor's, except where Chopin's is given in italics (see measures 23, 24, 36, 60, 81, 113, and 114).

Performance Suggestions

• Measures 1-3: Keep the melody and the harmony in perfect balance during the diminuendo, being careful not to stress notes played by the thumbs. The melody outlines a descending scale from the G-sharp of the opening chord to a G-sharp that we might imagine during the rest in measure 3. Avoid making a *ritard* or prolonging the rest, which would detract from the sense of anticipation left by the unresolved harmony. (The full tonic resolution comes on beats 5–7 of measure 4, where Chopin's pedaling holds the F-sharp major harmony.)

---

[30] Eric Heidsieck, "Dynamics or Motion? An Interpretation of Some Musical Signs in Romantic Piano Music," tr. Charles Timbrell, *Piano Quarterly* 140 (Winter 1987), 56-58; and Seymour Bernstein, *Chopin: Interpreting His Notational Symbols* (Milwaukee: Hal Leonard, 2005), 41-61.

[31] Frédéric Chopin: *Préludes*, Op. 28 and Op. 45, ed. Jean-Jacques Eigeldinger (New York: Peters, 2003), 61-62 ("Notes on Editorial Method and Practice"). See also Frédéric Chopin: *Ballades*, ed. Jan Ekier (Wiener Urtext Edition, 1986), preface.

- Measures 4–5: Play this figure in a simple, straightforward manner, *p* not *pp*. The evocation of lapping water is achieved by the rhythm as well as by the melodic contour.

- Starting at measure 14: The *leggiero* sixths should be unhurried and played with a light arm, the fingers close to the keys.

- Measures 15, 18, 22, 33, 111, and 112: Make subtle echo effects on the repeated phrases in these measures.

- Measure 32: A slight *ritard* is appropriate in this measure, which ends quietly (compare the different effect of the writing in measure 92).

- Measures 40–50: The indication *sotto voce* (in a low voice, subdued) applies to the two accompanying lines. Be sure that the melody sings out over them, and also in measures 44–50.

- Measures 43 and 47: Play the arpeggios freely and without a crescendo or final accent (compare the effect with the analogous measures 54, 58, and 60).

- Starting at measure 72: Play the chords *portato* (lightly released) rather than crisply staccato, to avoid a too-dry sound.

- Starting at measure 78: This special moment of musical intimacy, marked *sfogato* ("freely given out" or "with soft effusion"), should be played with a warm, singing tone, not *pp* or dulled by the *una corda* pedal.

- Measures 84–90: The left-hand octaves must sound smooth and light. Chopin's request to play them legato, which is hardly possible, should be understood to be an aural ideal. Keep the left arm loose, with the thumb close to the keys, and use shallow pedaling to help keep the hands in good balance.

- Measures 93–102: This magnificent climax should be played in an exalted manner, intensely but without ever forcing the sound. Shape the melodic line in the right hand, playing across the bar lines without accents. Practice the left-hand part for smooth position changes, always avoiding tension in the arm and shoulder. A change of color and slightly quieter dynamic is suggested for measures 96 (beat 10) to the middle of measure 99.

- 103-111: The harmonically rich polyphony of the coda may be projected at a somewhat slower tempo than Chopin's *tempo primo* marking, yet always moving forward. Many pianists have chosen to modify the indicated *sempre f* in order to explore a range of dynamic nuances and colors.

- Measure 115: Make an *accelerando* during the crescendo, changing the pedal as needed for clarity toward the end of the measure.

Dedicated to Madame la Baronne de Stockhausen

Barcarolle

Frédéric Chopin (1810–1849)
Op. 60

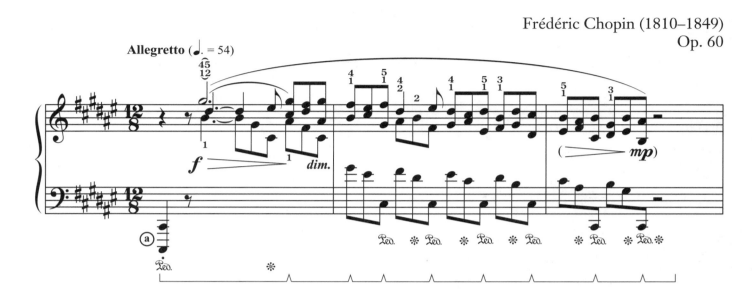

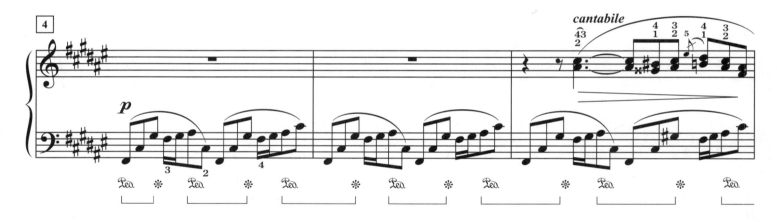

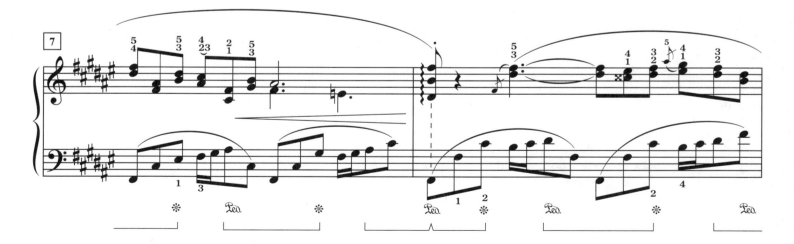

ⓐ Chopin's pedal indications for the introduction are not wholly satisfactory on modern instruments, since the opening octave—which is the root of the dominant-ninth harmony that underlies these measures—should not evaporate suddenly. This editor plays the octave *mf* and holds it with the sostenuto pedal until the last note of measure 3, during which time the damper pedal may be changed when the ear dictates, sometimes partially.

(e) On resonant instruments, it may be advisable to make shallow changes of the damper pedal in this passage of parallel sixths, and all similar places (i.e. measures 15, 18, 22, 33, 111, 112 and 115).

(n) In measures 34 and 51, Chopin's handwritten line connects the first grace note to the first bass note in the copy of the first French edition belonging to his student Camille Dubois (*née* O'Meara).

(o) Fingering in the Kraków autograph and first French edition:

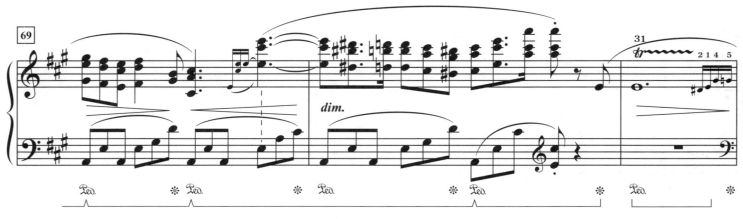

(p) This editor follows Mikuli, Joseffy, Debussy, Cortot and other editors in preferring a B-sharp on the 10th note; all the primary sources indicate a C-sharp.

ⓡ Alternate distribution for the last four chords:

ⓢ Alternate distribution for the last two chords:

Critical Commentary

Measure	Comment
1	*fz* on beat 1 in E only.
1-3	Slur in RH according to A1, E, and F; absent in A2 and G, where it begins in m. 2 and extends to the last note of m. 3.
1	G-sharps in RH tied in A1, A2, E, and G; in F the mark is interpreted as a slur extending from the first G-sharp to the following E-sharp.
1	Pedal release on beat 9 in A2 and G, after beat 8 in A1 and E, and on beat 8 in F.
2	Pedal according to all primary sources except G, where the first pedal indication extends from beats 1–5.
3	Pedal release according to A1, E, and F; absent in A2 and G.
6	Natural before the B on beat 10 in RH absent in A1, A2, and G; it is present in E and F (the latter possibly added in proofs).
8	Arpeggio mark on beat 1 in RH in A1, E, and F; absent in A2 and G.
8	Grace note before beat 10 in RH in A1, E, and F; absent in A2 and G.
9	Sharp on upper note on beat 12 in RH absent in all primary sources.
9	Crescendo sign missing in E only.
11	Ledger line missing on beat 10 in LH in F only (an obvious error), leading Mikuli and some other later editors to interpret the note as F-sharp.
11	Slurs in RH according to A2 and G; continuous slur from beat 4 in m. 10 to beat 1 in m. 12 in A1, E, and F.
11	Accent on the A-sharp on beat 4 in RH in A1 and F; absent in A2, E, and G.
11	Slurs in LH according to A1, A2, E, and G; slur on beats 1–7 in F (an obvious error) and slurs missing on beats 7–9 and 10–12 in F.

14	Accent on beat 4 in RH in A1 and A2 is interpreted as a diminuendo sign in E, F, and G.
14–17	Pedal indications according to A2, E, and G. In m. 14, the second pedal release is on beat 12 in A1 and F; in mm. 15–17 the pedal changes are on beats 1, 4, 7, and 10 in A1 and F.
15	Accent on beat 1 in RH in A1 and F; absent in all other primary sources.
17	Tie on beats 6 and 7 in LH in E only.
19	Beats 3 and 4 tied in LH in A1 and F; tie absent in all other primary sources.
20	Arpeggio mark on beat 10 in LH in A1, E, and F but absent on beat 9; arpeggio mark on beat 9 in LH in A2 and G but absent on beat 10.
20	Staccato on beat 1 in RH absent in A2, E, and G.
20	Staccato on beat 1 in LH absent in all sources.
20	Diminuendo sign on beats 3–6 in A2, E, and G; crescendo sign on beats 4–6 in A1 only, followed by a diminuendo sign on beats 7–9; crescendo sign on beats 1–3 in F only, followed by a diminuendo sign on beats 4–6 and another diminuendo sign on beats 7–9.
21	Diminuendo sign on beats 3–6 in A2 and G; accent on beats 3–4 in A1 and E; accent on beat 3 in F; crescendo sign on beats 4–6 in A1 and F, followed by a diminuendo sign on beats 7–9.
21	Staccato on beat 1 in RH absent in E only.
22	A-sharp in chord on beat 1 in RH absent in all primary sources (cf. m. 21).
22	Staccato on beat 1 in LH absent in A2, E, F, and G.
22	Staccato on beat 1 in RH absent in E and G.
22–26	Slur over RH in mm. 23–24 in A2 and G; slur from beat 9 in m. 22 to beat 1 in m. 26 in E; no slur over mm. 23–24 in A1 and F; slur from beat 7 in m. 24 to beat 1 in m. 26 in A1; slur ends on beat 12 in m. 25 in F and G (cf. the analogous passage mm. 6–8 and 84–86).
23–24	Chopin's fingering for the double trills in A1, A2, F, and G; absent in E.
24	*dim.* placed within the diminuendo sign in all primary sources.
24	Sharp on B on beat 8 in RH absent in A1 only.
24	Single grace note E-sharp before beat 10 in RH in A2, E, and G; grace note in thirds (C-sharp and E-sharp) in A1 and F.
24	Natural on B on beat 10 in RH in F and E.
24–25	Pedal from beat 12 in m. 24 to beat 3 in m. 25 in all primary sources, an apparent error originating in A1 and not corrected in the later sources (cf. mm. 6–7).
25	Diminuendo sign on beats 1–6 in A1 and F; absent in all other primary sources.
25	Pedal begins on beat 5 in A2 and G, on beat 6 in E, and on beat 7 in A1 and F.
26	Thirds on beat 10 in RH are quarter notes (without dots) in E only.
26	Thirds in the RH at the end of the measure are 16th notes in E only.
26–27	Pedal from beat 12 in m. 26 to beat 3 in m. 27 in A2 (an apparent copying error), E, and G (cf. mm. 24-25).
26–28	Slur over RH according to A2 and E; slur begins on beat 1 in m. 26 and ends on beat 12 in m. 27 in G; slur over beats 10–12 in m. 26 and separate slur over m. 27 in F; no slur in m. 26 in A1.
27	Diminuendo sign absent in A1 and F.

28	Accent on beat 4 in RH in A2. It appears to be a diminuendo sign in A1 and is so interpreted in E, F, and G.
29	Accent on beat 4 in RH missing in all primary sources. It appears to be a diminuendo sign in A1 and is so interpreted in F (but cf. the analogous passages mm. 28, 88, and 89).
31	Short diminuendo signs on beats 1 and 4 in RH in A1, A2, and G interpreted as accents in E and F.
31	*ten.* (*tenuto*) written over beats 1 and 4 in RH in A1 and F.
31	Slur over beats 4–6 in RH in A1, A2, E, and G; absent in F (added in FS).
31	Slur over beats 7 and 8 in RH in A1 and F.
31	G-sharp on beat 12 in RH lower voice absent in A2 and G.
32	Slur begins on beat 1 in RH in F and E.
32	Slur missing in LH in all sources.
32	Chords on beats 10 and 11 in RH according to F (possibly changed in proofs); chords in all other primary sources contain a B.
32	*dim.* written within the diminuendo sign in A2; *dim.* above the diminuendo sign in E and G; *dim.* only in A1 and F.
33	Slurred staccato marks on beats 2–11 in LH missing in all sources.
33	Grace note C-sharp on beat 1 in RH absent in F only.
33	Pedal indications according to A2, E, and G. Changes of pedal occur on beats 1, 4, 7 and 10 in A1 and F.
34	Grace note on beat 1 in RH linked by handwritten line to first note in LH in FD.
34	Pedal according to A2 and G; pedal from beats 1–8 in A1 and F, and from beats 1–12 in W. There is a second pedal marking from beats 9–11 in A1 and F.

34–35	Slurs according to A2 and G; slur from beat 1 in m. 34 to beat 1 in m. 35 in A1, E, and F.
35	*Poco più mosso* begins on beat 5 in A1 and A2, on beat 4 in F and G, and on beat 7 in E.
36	Chopin's fingering in A1 and F: 2 on beats 7 and 10 (downward stems indicate LH), 4 on beat 8 (RH), 2 on beat 9 (RH), 5 on beat 11 (RH); absent in all other primary sources.
38	Short diminuendo sign over beats 10 and 11 in RH in A1 interpreted as an accent in F; no sign in A2, E, and G.
38	Both B's on beat 10 are double stemmed in A1, A2, and G; single stemmed in E and F.
40	Upper A on beat 1 in RH tied from m. 39 in A1 and F.
40–41	Crescendo sign in F, evidently added in proofs (cf. the analogous passage mm. 43–44 in A2 and G).
41	New slur on beats 4–6 in RH upper voice in E only.
41–42	Diminuendo sign from beats 10–12 in RH upper voice in m. 41 to beat 4 in m. 42 in A2, E, and G; given as an accent on beat 10 in RH upper voice in m. 41 in A1 and F.
41–42	Tie from last C-sharp in RH upper voice in m. 45 to first C-sharp absent in all primary sources (cf. mm. 45-46).
40–42	New slur from beat 7 in RH upper voice in m. 41 to beat 12 of m. 42 in E only, and similarly in mm. 45–46. In all other sources, the slur extends from m. 40 to the end of m. 42 (but cf. the analogous passage mm. 44–46).
42	Slur under beats 7–12 in RH lower voice in A1 and F; absent in A2, E, and G (but cf. the analogous passage in m. 46 in A1, A2, F, and G).
43	Pedal release according to A1, E, and F; absent in A2 and G.

43–44 No crescendo sign in A1, E, and F. The crescendo in A2 (probably a copying error) and G contradicts the *sempre **p*** indication in all primary sources.

43–44, 46–47 Staccato on beat 1 in LH in A1 only.

45–46 New slur begins on beat 7 in RH upper voice in m. 45 in E only. In all other sources, the new slur begins on beat 10 and extends to beat 12 of m. 46 (but cf. the analogous passage mm. 40-42).

45–46 Tie from last B in RH upper voice in m. 45 to first B in m. 46 in A1 and F; tie absent in all other primary sources.

45–46 Diminuendo sign absent in A2 and G, should probably match that in mm. 41–42 in A2, E, and G.

46 Octave on beat 1 in LH in A1 and F; lower note only in all other primary sources.

46–47 Slur from beat 12 in LH in m. 46 to beat 1 in m. 47 in A1, E, F; absent in A2 and G.

47–48 Slur in RH according to A1, A2, and G; absent in F (added in FS). Separate slur on beats 5–8 in m. 47 in E; no slur on beats 7–9 in m. 48 in E.

48 G-sharp on beat 3 in RH lower voice in A2 and G; F♯ in A1, E, and F (cf. m. 59).

48 Slur from D on beat 1 to C-sharp on beat 7 in RH in A2 and G; absent in A1, E, and F.

48 Diminuendo sign absent in F.

50 *cresc.* placed within the crescendo sign in A1, A2, F, and G; above the sign in E.

50 Sharp on the second grace note in RH absent in all primary sources (cf. beat 11 in RH, below).

50 Sharp on D on beat 8 in RH absent in all primary sources except F (evidently added in proofs).

50 Natural on D on beat 11 in RH in F only.

50 Natural on D on beat 12 in RH absent in all primary sources except F (evidently added in proofs).

51 Grace-note chord in RH linked by handwritten line to first note in LH in FD.

51 A in the grace-note chord in RH absent in E.

51 ***f*** is placed on the downbeat in all primary sources (cf. m. 55).

51 Single note on beat 1 in LH in A2, E, and G; octave in A1 and F.

51–53 Slurs in RH according to A2, E, and G; one slur over mm. 51–53 in A1 and F.

52 Crescendo sign absent in all primary sources (but cf. the analogous passage m. 56 in A2 and G).

53 Pedal changes on beats 6 and 9 in all primary sources, possibly an error originating in A1 and not corrected in the later sources (cf. the analogous passage m. 57 in A1, E, and F).

54 *cresc.* placed within the crescendo sign in A2, E, and G; under the sign in A1 and F.

54 Notes 1–8 in RH according to A1 and F; note 6 is B in A2 and E, B-sharp in G.

54 ***fzp*** on beat 4 in RH in A2 and E; ***fp*** on beat 4 in G; no marking on beat 4 and ***p*** on beat 5 in A1 and F.

55 Slur from m. 54 in RH ends on beat 1 in A1 and A2.

55 ***f*** on beat 1 in A1 and F, on beat 2 in A2, E, and G (cf. m. 51).

55–57 Slurs in LH absent in all primary sources (but cf. the analogous passage mm. 51-53).

55 Sharp above the trill absent in all primary sources.

55 Slur over beats 2–6 in RH absent in all primary sources except E.

55 Pedal release on beat 7 absent in A2 and G.

56 Pedal according to A1 and F; pedal absent on beats 4–6 in all other primary sources.

56 Octave G on beat 7 in LH in A1, E, and F; upper G only in A2 and G.

57 Tie on bottom notes of beats 6–7 in RH absent in all primary sources except G (but cf. the analogous passage m. 53).

57 Diminuendo sign on beats 7–9 in RH in A1, E, and F; absent in A2 and G.

57 Pedal indication according to A2 and G. Pedal on beats 7–9 in A1, E, and F (but cf. the analogous passage m. 53 in A2 and G).

57 Slur on beats 10–12 in RH according to A1, E, and F; absent in A2 and G.

58 *fzp* on beat 4 in RH in A2 and E; *fp* on beat 4 in G; no marking on beat 4 and *p* on beat 5 in A1 and F.

58 No dynamic marks on beats 7–12 in A2 and G; *cresc.* together with crescendo sign on these beats in A1, E, and F.

59 *cresc.* beginning on beat 9 in A2 and G; absent in other primary sources.

59 Slur on beats 1–6 in RH in E; on beats 1–7 in A1, A2, F, and G.

59 Slur begins on beat 8 in RH in A2 and G; on beat 9 in A1; on beat 7 in E; no slur on second half of the measure in F (added in FS, extending from beat 10 in m. 59 to beat 6 in m. 60).

59 G-sharp on beat 3 in RH lower voice in A2, E, and G; F-sharp in A1 and F (cf. m. 48).

59 Octave on beat 12 in LH in A2 (apparent copying error) and G.

60 Accent on beat 1 in RH in A1, E, and F; possibly a diminuendo sign in A2 and so interpreted in G.

60 Chopin's fingering on notes 7 and 9 in RH lower voice in A1 and F: 1, 4; absent in all other primary sources.

60–61 Slur from beat 12 in m. 60 to beat 3 in m. 61 in RH in A2 and G; to beat 12 in m. 61 in A1 and F; to beat 6 in E.

61 Crescendo sign together with prolongation dashes that extend from *cresc.* in m. 59 in A2; crescendo sign only in A1, F, and G; no crescendo sign in E.

61–62 New slur from beat 7 in m. 61 to beat 1 in m. 62 in RH in E only.

61 New slur on beats 1–6 in LH in A1 and F; slur continues from m. 60 to beat 6 in m. 61 in E; slur absent in A2 and G.

61 Slur on beats 7–10 in LH in E only.

61 Accent on beat 4 in RH upper voice in A1, E, and F; absent in A2 and G.

61 *ritenuto* placed according to A1, A2, and E; placed beginning on beat 3 in F and on beat 4 in G.

62 Slurs in RH according to A2 and G; slur on beats 3-12 in E; continuous slur from beat 1 in m. 62 through beat 7 in m. 63 in A1 and F.

63 Pedal indications according to A2, E, and G. Pedals begin on beats 2 and 8 in F, on beat 3 and 7 in A1.

63, 65 Ties on last chord in RH absent in E.

65 Diminuendo sign on beats 10–12 in A1 and F; crescendo sign A2 and G; marking absent in E.

66 Crescendo sign on beats 1–5 in A1 and F; absent in all other primary sources.

66 Ties on beats 3–4 in RH absent in E.

67 Octave E's on beat 1 in RH tied from m. 66 in A1 and F.

67–69 Slur in RH continuous in A1 and F; new slur begins on beat 9 of m. 68 in A2 (possible oversight), E, and G.

69 Crescendo sign absent in A1, E, and F.

70 Staccato on beat 10 in RH in A2 and G; absent in A1, E, and F.

70 Staccato on beat 10 in LH absent in all primary sources.

71 Fermata over the trill added by Chopin in FD.

71–72 Pedal ends at the end of m. 71 in E, on beat 1 in m. 72 in A1 and F, and is absent entirely in A2 (possibly a copying oversight) and G.

72 Pedal on beats 1–3 in E only and on beats 6–7 in G only; pedal on beats 7–9 in all other primary sources.

72 *p* absent in A2 (possibly a copying oversight) and G.

72 Staccatos on beats 3, 4, 6, and 7 in LH absent in G.

72 Staccatos on beats 9, 10, and 12 in LH in A1, A2, E, and G; absent on beats 10 and 12 in F.

72 Pedal according to A1, A2, and F; pedal on beats 7–12 in E; pedal on beats 6–8 in G.

73 Pedal on beats 1–3 according to A2, E, and G; pedal release absent in A1 and F.

73 Pedal on beats 7–9 according to A1 and A2; pedal on beats 7–8 and 9–10 in E; pedal on beats 7–8 in F and G.

73 Accent on beat 3 in RH in A1; diminuendo sign possibly in A2 and so interpreted in E and G; no marking in F.

74 Accent on beat 3 in RH in A1, E, F, and G; diminuendo sign possibly in A2.

75 Accent on beats 1 and 9 in RH in A2, E, and G; diminuendo signs possibly in A1 and F.

75 Slur ends on beat 7 in RH and new slur begins on beat 9 according to A2 and G; one continuous slur in A1 and F, ending on beat 12; no slur on beats 9–12 in E.

The salon at Nohant where Chopin composed the Barcarolle

75 Tie on first two F-naturals in RH in A1, E, and F; absent in A2 (probably a copying oversight) and G.

76 Diminuendo sign absent in A2 and G.

76 Octave C-sharp on beat 1 in LH in A2, E, and G; octave D in A1 and F.

76 Sharp before the last note in LH in F (evidently corrected in proofs).

77 Diminuendo sign absent in A2 and G.

77 Pedal absent in A1 and F.

78 Sharp on last F in RH absent in all primary sources except F (evidently added in proofs).

78 Pedal ends after beat 10 in A2, E, and G, after beat 7 in A1 and F.

78–82 Long slur in RH according to A1. In m. 80, a new slur begins on beat 1 in F (possibly because m. 80 begins a new page), on beat 3 in A2 and G, and on beat 4 in E.

81 C-sharp on beat 10 in RH in all primary sources. Mikuli, Joseffy, Debussy, Cortot, and others have suggested that Chopin may have intended a B-sharp, as on beats 3, 9, and 11.

81	Chopin's fingering (thumb) for notes 3, 9, and 15 in RH in A1; on notes 9 and 15 in F; absent in all other primary sources.
83	Slur on beats 1–6 in RH in A1, E, and F.
83	Natural on beat 10 in RH lower note absent in A2 and E.
83	Sharp on beat 11 in RH lower voice absent in all primary sources except F (evidently added in proofs).
83	C-sharp on beat 5 in LH absent in G.
84	Ties from beats 1–7 in RH in A1 and F; ties absent in all other primary sources (cf. ties present in m. 6 in all sources).
84–87	Slurs in LH according to A1, E, and F. In A2 and G the slurs are under beats 2–5 and beats 8–11.
84, 86	Pedal according to A2, E, and G. Pedal absent on beats 7–9 but present on beats 11–12 in A1 and F.
86	Ties on chords 2–3 in RH absent in A2 and G.
88	Unclosed diminuendo sign (an obvious error) on beats 1 and 2 in G; continuation of the crescendo sign from m. 87 in all other primary sources.
88, 89	Slurs under beats 7–9 and 10–12 in LH in E; absent in all other primary sources.
89	Ties in RH according to A2, E, and F (possibly added in proofs), and G; absent in A1.
90	Accent on beat 1 in RH absent in A1, E, and F.
90	Arpeggio mark on beat 7 in RH in A1, E, and F; absent in A2 and G.
90, 91	Slurs in LH absent in all primary sources (cf. mm. 30-31).
91	Ornament is *tr* in A2, E, and G; is 〰 in A1 and F.
92	Slur on beat 12 in LH absent in all primary sources.

92	Top note on beat 7 in LH is F-sharp in A1, A2, E, and G. It is G-sharp in F (deleted in FS).
92	Top note on beat 8 in LH is A-sharp in A1 and F; in all other primary sources it is F-sharp, which is a more practical stretch although it breaks the pattern of top-note doublings between the hands throughout the measure.
92	Slur on beats 2–11 in RH according to A2 and G.
93	Slurs in RH according to A2 and G; continuous slur in A1 and F; new slur begins on beat 7 in E.
94–95	Ties from the C-sharps in RH on beat 10 in m. 94 to those on beat 1 in m. 95 are absent in all primary sources. Some editors have added them because of a similar passage in mm. 63–64, but in the earlier passage there is no change of harmony and the dynamic is much softer.
95	C-sharp in chord on beat 6 in LH in A1 and F; absent in A2, E, and G.
95	Chord on beat 8 in LH is A-sharp, C-sharp, F-sharp in A1, E, and F (cf. identical pattern in m. 93); it is C-sharp, F-sharp, A-sharp in A2 (evidently a copying error) and G.
96	Chord on beat 3 in LH is G-sharp, B, E-sharp in A2 and G; G-sharp, B, C-sharp, E-sharp in A1, E, and F.
96	Chord on beat 5 in LH according to A1, A2, E, and G; added A-sharp in F (deleted in FS).
96	Diminuendo sign on beats 10–12 in A1, E, and F; absent in A2 and G.
96–100	Slur continuous in RH in A2 and G; new slurs begin on beat 1 in m. 98 and on beat 9 in m. 99 in A1 and F; on beat 7 in m. 97, beat 1 in m. 98, and beat 9 in m. 99 in E.
98	Octave F-sharp on beats 6–7 in RH tied in A1, E, and F; absent in A2 and G.

100	Last chord in RH tied to beat 1 of m. 101 in F (evidently added in proofs).
100	Accent on beat 10 in RH in A2 and G interpreted as a diminuendo sign in E; crescendo sign on beats 10–12 in A1 and F.
101	Middle note on beat 7 in RH is F-sharp in A2 and G; C-sharp in A1, E, and F.
102	*ten.* (*tenuto*) over trill in A1 and F.
102	Pedal release before beat 7 in A1, A2, and G, and on beat 3 in E; pedal release absent in F.
102	Pedal indication on beats 7–9 in A2, E, and G; on beats 7–8 in A1; on beats 10–12 in F.
102	Diminuendo sign in A2, E, and G; absent in A1 and F.
102	Termination of trill (F-double-sharp) added editorially.
102	Top note on beat 11 in LH is G-sharp in G only.
102	Natural on bottom note on beat 11 in LH in F; sharp in G; no sign in A1, A2, and E.
102–103	Slurs in RH according to Chopin's changes in FD. Slur over beats 11 and 12 in A1 and F; slur over beats 8–12 in E; slur over beats 8–12 ends on beat 1 of m. 103 in A2 and G.
103	Slur begins on beat 4 in RH in A2 and G, on beat 1 in A1, E, and F.
103	*sempre* **f** in A2, E, and G; **f** only in A1 and F.
103	*tempo primo* in E and F; absent in A2 and G; mm. 103–104 partially missing in A1.
104	F-sharp in chord on beat 10 in RH in E and F; absent in A2 and G; m. 104 partially missing in A1.
105	Arpeggio mark on beat 1 in RH absent in all primary sources.
105	Accents on beats 1 and 4 in RH absent in A1 and F.
105	Diminuendo sign absent in all primary sources.
105	Natural on A on beat 11 in LH absent in A2 and G.
105	Upper slur in RH according to A1, A2, and G; absent in F; upper slurs only on beats 7–9 and 10–12 in E .
107	*sempre* **f** in A1 and F; absent in all other primary sources.
107	Accents on beats 1 and 4 in RH in A2, E, and G; absent in A1 and F.
107	Pedal according to A1 and F; pedal absent on beats 4–6 in A2, E, and G.
107	Lower note on beat 6 in RH is F in G.
107	Natural on top note on beat 9 in LH absent in A2 and G; absent in all other primary sources.
107	Natural on beat 12 in RH absent in A1, A2, and G.
108	Accents on beats 1 and 4 in RH in A2, E, and G; absent in A1 and F.
108	D-natural on upper note on beat 6 in RH in A1, E, and F; C-double-sharp in A2 and G. There is no source known for the C-sharp given in later editions by Cortot, Debussy, Diémer, Friedman, Gambaryan, Joseffy, and Sauer.
108	Natural on B on beat 10 in RH absent in all primary sources.
108	Natural on beat 12 in RH absent in all primary sources except F.
109	Accents on beats 1 and 4 in RH in A2, E, and G; absent in A1 and F.
109	Arpeggio mark on beat 1 in RH absent in all primary sources.
109	Middle note in chord on beat 4 in LH is B in A1, E, and F; A-sharp in A2 and G.

110   *fz* on beat 1 in A2, E and G; absent in A1 and F.

110   Slur in LH begins on beat 1 in E and G, on beat 2 in all other primary sources.

110   Slur in LH ends on beat 4 in E only.

110   Double-sharp on third F in RH absent in A2, E, and G.

110   Natural absent on third note in RH in all primary sources.

110   Sharp absent on fifth note in RH in all primary sources.

110   Sharp absent on last three E's in RH in all primary sources (but not strictly necessary).

111   Single note on beat 1 in LH in A2, E, and G; octave in A1 and F.

112   *dim.* in A1, A2, F, and G; absent in E.

113   Chopin's fingering at beginning of beats 8 and 9 in RH in A1 only: 1, 4.

113   Natural missing on beat 11 in RH in all primary sources.

114   Beat 6 in LH according to A1, A2, E, and G. The A-sharp is missing in F (added in FS).

114   Beat 7 in LH according to A1, A2, F, and G. The C-sharp is missing in E.

114   Chopin's fingering on penultimate A-sharp and B in RH in A1 only: 4, 1.

114   Chopin's fingering on last note in RH in A1 only: 1.

114   Pedal indications absent in A2, E, and G; pedal on beats 3–5, 6–9, and 10–12 in A1 and F.

115   Pedal release according to A2 and G; on the 16th note from the end of the measure (F-sharp) in E; on the last note in A1 and F.

115   Sixth note from the end of the scale is E-sharp in A2, E, and G. This note is missing in A1 and F.

116   *ff* on beat 1 in A1, A2, and E; over beat 2 in F and G.

116   Pedal according to A2, E, and G. No pedal on beat 1 in A1 and F; pedal on each pair of octaves in A1 and F.

116   Final pedal release according to E and G; absent in A1, A2, and F.